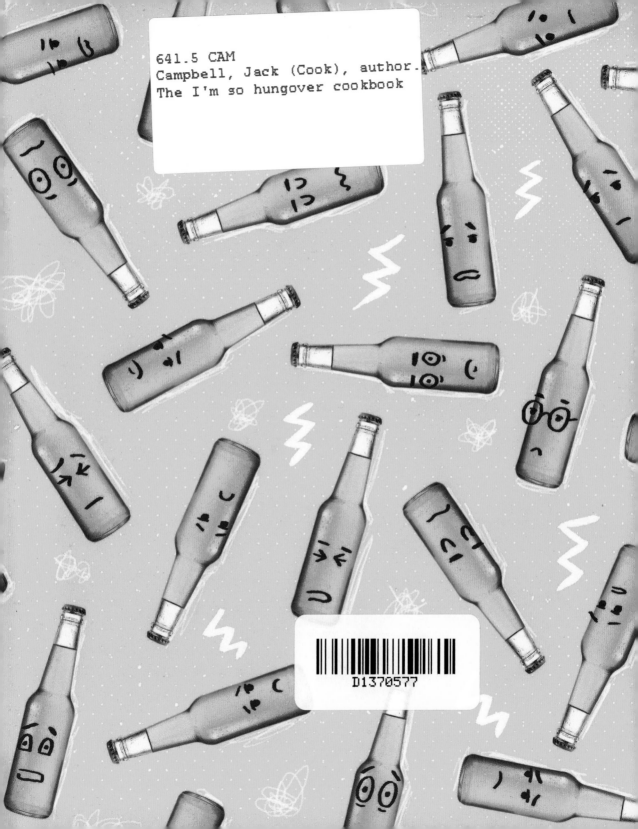

THE I'M SO HUNG OVER COOKBOOK

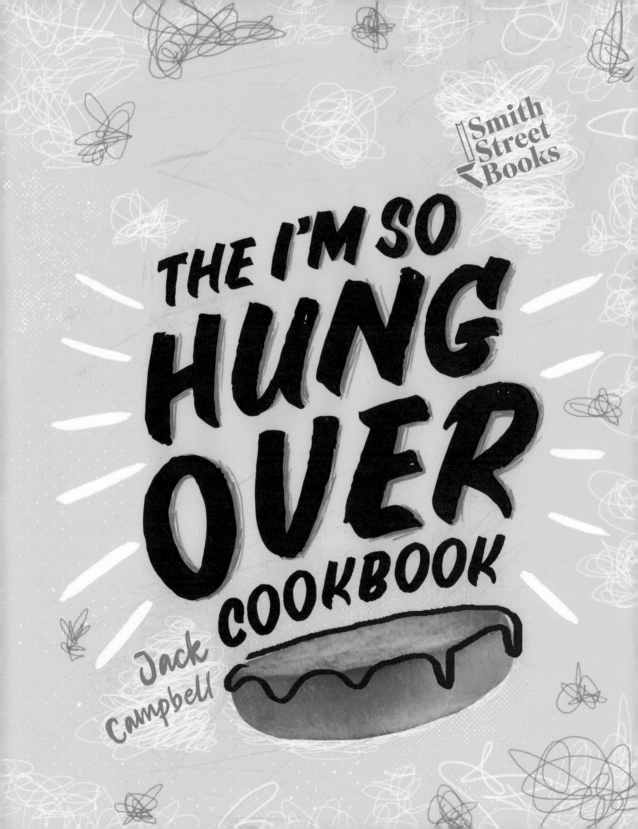

CONTENTS

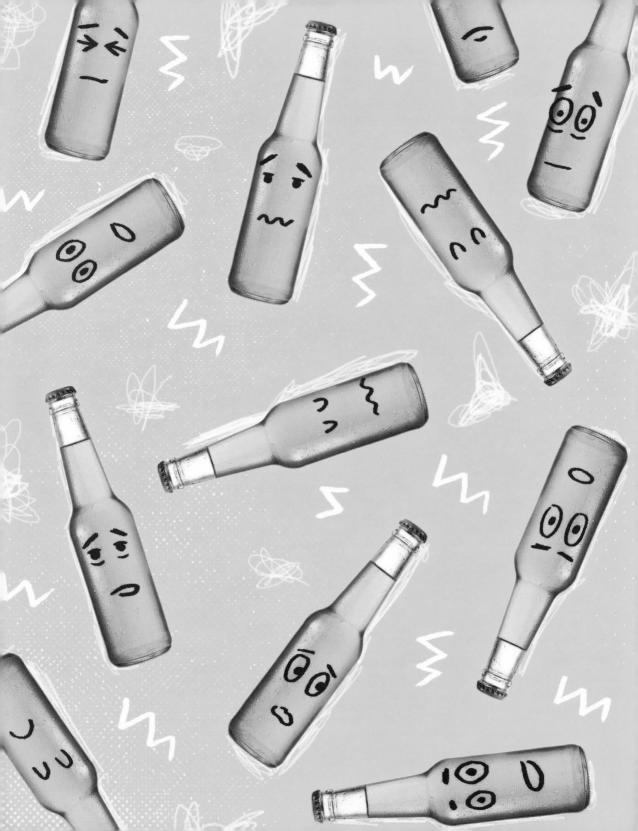

INTRODUCTION

At present, science can't tell us much about hangovers. There remain many unanswered questions: why do hangovers happen? Why do they seem to correlate with my patterns of heavy drinking? Has anyone seen my passport?

The only thing that modern 'science' has actually proven, is that greasy and otherwise carbohydrate-heavy foods seem to mystically alleviate the symptoms of this condition. It's for this reason I've created a resource for all the hungover and haggard among us.

The chapters in this book are structured to correspond to your precise degree of hungover-ness. Chapter 1: Shaky, But Standing is there for the ambitious kitchen cretin. There will be some actual cooking involved and, if you can manage that, the payoff will be delicious. The chapters generally decrease in difficulty until we get to Chapter 4: Beyond Salvation, which is more palliative than it is productive.

One might reasonably argue that a hangover is not the right state of mind in which to cook food. The recipes here (especially those in the first two chapters) may require some pleading to a housemate or long-suffering life partner to prepare them for you. Or if you're heading for a big night, why not plan ahead and cook up a batch of something so there's no need to make any decisions in your fragile state other than which Bruce Willis movie to watch.

Whatever the severity of your dustiness, take comfort in these 50 dishes and the knowledge that all across the world there are people, just like yourself, for whom today's struggle is real.

Also, you should probably hydrate.

CHAPTER 1:
SHAKY, BUT STANDING

So, your after-work drinks escalated? A few beers on an empty stomach?

Oh yeah, those IPAs will sneak up on you. We have all made this

mistake on a weeknight, you are going to be just fine.

All you need is some salty, greasy, carby food

and you can get to work on time

and keep your eyes open (enough).

DANK BREAKFAST BURRITO

SERVES 2

INGREDIENTS

2 free-range eggs
a splash of milk
olive oil, for frying
2 teaspoons butter
4 large mushrooms, thickly sliced
2 bacon slices (omit for a veggie
    version)
2 large flour tortillas
2 dollops Guacamole (page 109)
2 tablespoons pickled jalapeños
hot sauce of your choice
handful of coriander (cilantro),
    roughly chopped
½ lime

METHOD

Whisk the eggs with the milk in a small bowl and season with salt and pepper. Set aside.

Heat a little olive oil and half the butter in a small saucepan over medium heat. Add the mushrooms and stir to coat. Season with salt and pepper, reduce the heat to low and cook slowly for about 10 minutes until the liquid has evaporated and the mushrooms are starting to brown.

Meanwhile, heat 1 teaspoon of oil in a frying pan over medium heat and add the bacon. Cook until crisp.

Heat the remaining butter in a small saucepan over low heat. Add the egg mixture and cook for 2–3 minutes, stirring constantly, until scrambled. Remove from the heat.

Heat each tortilla in a large dry frying pan over medium heat for about 1 minute on each side until soft and warmed through.

Preheat a sandwich press.

Spoon the scrambled egg onto one side of each tortilla and place the bacon on top. Add the mushrooms, guacamole, jalapeños and as much hot sauce as you can handle. Finish with the coriander and a good squeeze of lime.

Fold up the bottom end of each tortilla, then carefully fold over the shorter side and roll up. Toast the burrito in the sandwich press for 2–3 minutes until just starting to brown. (Spillages are subject to filling to tortilla ratio.)

It was hungover Californians
who first realised you can eat
anything for breakfast, if you put
the word breakfast in the recipe title.

BACON > PAINKILLERS

FARMER'S BREAKFAST

SERVES 2

*True, the only toiling you did last night was on the dancefloor.
But that doesn't mean you don't deserve this German-inspired Farmer's feast.*

INGREDIENTS

3 medium-sized potatoes (about
    300 g/10½ oz), peeled
1 teaspoon olive oil
150 g (5½ oz) bacon, cut into
    thin strips
1 green capsicum (bell pepper),
    chopped
4 free-range eggs
½ bunch chives, snipped

METHOD

Place the potatoes in a saucepan and cover with
water. Season with salt, then bring to the boil and
cook for 15 minutes or until a knife slips through the
flesh easily. Drain, allow to cool slightly, then slice the
potatoes into rounds about 1 cm (½ in) thick.

Heat the olive oil in a large frying pan over medium–
high heat and add the bacon and capsicum. Cook until
the bacon is crisp and the capsicum is soft. Push the
bacon and capsicum to one side of the pan, then add
the sliced potato. Cook for 4–5 minutes on each side
until lightly browned. Mix through the bacon and
capsicum until the ingredients are evenly dispersed
around the pan.

Preheat the grill (broiler) to high.

Whisk the eggs in a small bowl and season with salt
and pepper. Pour into the pan and swirl, so that the
egg evenly settles between the other ingredients.
Reduce the heat to low, cover with a lid and cook for
3–5 minutes, until the egg is just set. Transfer the
pan to the hot grill and cook for 3–4 minutes until
brown on top. Garnish with the chopped chives and
serve immediately.

OKONOMIYAKI

MAKES 8

Trying to pronounce this Japanese pancake while hungover is a struggle indeed.

INGREDIENTS

150 g (5½ oz/1 cup) plain
   (all-purpose) flour
40 g (1½ oz/⅓ cup) cornflour
   (corn starch)
¼ teaspoon salt
¼ teaspoon sugar
¼ teaspoon baking powder
185 ml (6 fl oz/¾ cup) vegetable stock
4 free-range eggs
¼ cup pickled red ginger, plus extra
   to garnish
½ medium white or savoy cabbage,
   thinly sliced
Okonomi sauce (see note), to serve
Japanese (Kewpie) mayo, to serve
8 spring onions (scallions), finely
   chopped

NOTE
Okonomi sauce is available from Asian grocery stores. A quick substitute sauce can be made by blending 3 tablespoons tomato ketchup, 1 tablespoon vegetarian worcestershire sauce, 1 tablespoon mushroom soy sauce and 2 teaspoons of sugar.

METHOD

In a large bowl, combine the flour, cornflour, salt, sugar and baking powder. Add the stock, whisk well and refrigerate the batter for 1 hour.

Preheat a hooded barbecue hotplate (griddle) to medium and lightly grease with oil.

Add the eggs and pickled ginger to the batter and mix well. Stir in the cabbage.

Spoon ladles of batter onto the oiled hotplate to make eight pancakes. Cover and cook for 5 minutes until browned on the bottom. (The cover helps the thick pancake cook through to the centre.) Turn, cover and cook for 5 minutes until browned. Turn once more and cook, uncovered, for another 2 minutes.

To serve, drizzle with Okonomi sauce and Japanese mayo and garnish with spring onion and extra pickled ginger.

When potato
is life

POTATO & BACON BAKE

SERVES 4

On a day like today, a wake and bake might be just what you need.

INGREDIENTS

1 tablespoon olive oil
20 g (¾ oz) butter
200 g (7 oz) bacon, cut into strips
1 leek, pale part only, thinly sliced
1 kg (2 lb 3 oz) potatoes, thinly sliced
2 garlic cloves, thinly sliced
400 ml (13½ fl oz) thickened
    (whipping) cream (35% fat)
25 g (1 oz/¼ cup) grated parmesan
    cheese
1 spring onion (scallion), thinly sliced

METHOD

Preheat the oven to 160°C/320°F (fan-forced). Lightly grease a large roasting pan or baking dish.

Heat the oil and butter in a large heavy-based lidded frying pan over medium heat. Add the bacon and cook, stirring, for 6–8 minutes until crisp. Remove with a slotted spoon and drain on paper towel. Set aside.

Add the leek to the same pan and cook, stirring, for 4–5 minutes until tender. Add the potato, garlic and cream, season well and bring to the boil, stirring gently. Cover and simmer for 8–10 minutes until the potato is just starting to soften.

Remove from the heat and carefully spoon into the prepared pan. Scatter with the bacon, poking it between the potato slices in a few places. Sprinkle with the cheese.

Bake for 25–30 minutes until tender and golden. If the top begins to brown too much, cover with foil. Remove from the oven and rest for 5 minutes. Serve scattered with the spring onion.

BACON 'SALAD'

SERVES 4

INGREDIENTS

4 bacon slices
2 teaspoons white vinegar
4 large very fresh free-range eggs
2 baby cos (romaine) lettuces,
    leaves separated
1 avocado, sliced
chopped fresh herbs, to serve
200ml jar of premade hollandaise
    sauce

POTATO NUGGETS

500 g (1 lb 2 oz) waxy potatoes
    (such as desiree), quartered
½ small onion, grated
1 teaspoon plain (all-purpose) flour
¼ teaspoon salt
peanut oil, for deep-frying

NOTE

Look, no one will judge you if you want to simplify things here and use some premade frozen potato gems (tater tots) instead of making your own potato nuggets. Just cook according to the packet instructions.

METHOD

For the potato nuggets, place the potatoes in a large saucepan and cover with cold water. Bring to the boil and simmer for 8–10 minutes or until barely tender. Drain the potatoes and allow to cool a little, then peel and coarsely grate. The potato should be quite sticky. Gently place in a large bowl along with the onion, flour and salt. Season with pepper and mix with a fork.

Preheat the oven to 140°C/275°F (fan-forced). Line a large baking tray with baking paper.

Heat the oil in a deep saucepan or deep-fryer to 180°C (350°F). A crumb added to the oil should sizzle immediately. Roll heaped teaspoons of the potato mixture gently into oval shapes. Fry in batches of 4–5 at a time for 3–4 minutes until golden brown. Drain on paper towel and keep warm in the oven on the prepared tray.

Put the bacon in a heavy-based frying pan and place over medium–high heat. Cook for about 3 minutes on each side.

Meanwhile, fill a deep frying pan with boiling water. Bring to a light simmer over medium heat and add the vinegar. Crack one of the eggs into a cup and gently pour it into the water in one fluid movement. Repeat with the rest of the eggs. Cook for 3–4 minutes, until the whites are set, but the yolks still runny.

Divide the lettuce among four plates. Top with the avocado, bacon, poached eggs and potato nuggets. Drizzle with the hollandaise and sprinkle with herbs. Serve immediately.

This is as close as you will come to a salad today.

HANGOVER CURES AROUND THE WORLD

SCOTLAND
The 'Highland Fling' is a restorative pint of buttermilk, heated and blended with a tablespoon of cornflour (corn starch). Season to taste.

PUERTO RICO
Drinkers here believe rubbing a slice of **lemon** under their armpits before drinking, might prevent sweating and thus ensuring no hangover from dehydration.

MONGOLIA
We've all forced down a bloody mary (page 115) at breakfast, but Mongolians take it to another level by mixing tomato juice and **pickled sheep eyeballs.** What an eye opener.

HAITI
Voodoo-ers stick 13 black-headed **pins** into the cork of the bottle from which they received a hangover. It seems that canned beverages are spared from this pointy punishment.

SICILY
Although this hangover remedy is oddly fading in popularity, Sicilians have been known to nibble on a... **dried bull's penis...** to clear their heads.

JAPAN
The most wholesome treatment of all comes from the Japanese, who suggest dissolving a **pickled plum** in your mouth for at least half an hour.

THE WILD WEST
American cowboys would supposedly brew up some 'pellet tea' to recoup after a night on the moonshine. That would be **rabbit poo** steeped in boiling water. **Yee-haw** or **yee-uck?**

Savoury pies for your
unsavoury morning.

CHICKEN POT PIE

SERVES 4

INGREDIENTS

1 tablespoon olive oil

700 g (1 lb 9 oz) skinless chicken thigh
fillets, cut into chunks

2 leeks, pale part only, halved
lengthways and chopped

1 medium–large carrot, chopped

1 celery stalk, chopped

1 large garlic clove, finely chopped

3 lemon thyme or thyme sprigs

1 bay leaf

125 ml (4 fl oz/½ cup) dry white wine

250 ml (8½ fl oz/1 cup) chicken stock

185 ml (6½ fl oz/¾ cup) thickened
(whipping) cream (35% fat)

1 teaspoon dijon mustard

1 tablespoon chopped tarragon
or sage

50 g (1¾ oz) English spinach,
shredded

1 egg, beaten

2 sheets frozen puff pastry, thawed

METHOD

Heat the oil in a saucepan and brown the chicken over
high heat for 8–10 minutes. Add the leek, carrot, celery
and garlic and cook over medium heat for 5 minutes,
or until the vegetables soften. Add the thyme and bay
leaf and season with salt and pepper. Stir in the wine
and cook for 2–3 minutes, or until reduced by half,
then add the stock. Cover and leave to cook over low
heat for 45 minutes.

Remove the lid from the pan. Stir in the cream and
simmer gently for a further 25 minutes. Remove and
discard the thyme and bay leaf. Stir in the mustard and
tarragon, then stir the spinach through until wilted.
Remove from the heat and leave to cool.

Preheat the oven to 180°C/350°F (fan-forced).

Divide the chicken mixture among four 250 ml
(8½ fl oz/1 cup) ramekins. Brush around the rim with
beaten egg, so the pastry will adhere. Place a ramekin
on the thawed pastry and cut out a circle a bit larger
than the ramekin. Place the pastry over the filling,
pressing the dough down around the outside of the
ramekin. Repeat with the remaining pastry, until all
the pies are topped. Using a knife, make a small slit in
the centre of each pie lid, to allow steam to escape.

Bake for 30 minutes, or until the pastry is golden and
puffed. Serve hot.

EASY CHIPOTLE CHILLI CON CARNE

SERVES 4

INGREDIENTS

2 tablespoons olive oil
1 red onion, finely chopped
2 garlic cloves, crushed
1 fresh Mexican chorizo sausage,
    skin removed
1 teaspoon ground cumin
1 teaspoon smoked paprika
1 tinned chipotle chilli in
    adobo sauce, chopped
1 bay leaf
400 g (14 oz) tinned crushed tomatoes
125 ml (4 fl oz/½ cup) beef stock
500 g (1 lb 2 oz) stewing steak, cut
    into large cubes
110 g (4 oz/½ cup) dried black beans,
    rinsed
juice of 1 lime
2 squares dark chocolate
1 handful coriander (cilantro), leaves
    and stalk chopped, plus extra
    leaves to serve
1 tomato, chopped
1 avocado, chopped
cooked white rice, to serve

METHOD

Heat the olive oil in a large heavy-based saucepan over medium heat. Add the onion and garlic and cook for 3 minutes, or until softened. Crumble the chorizo into the pan, add the cumin and paprika and cook, stirring, for 2–3 minutes, until the chorizo is cooked.

Stir in the chipotle chilli, bay leaf, tomatoes and stock and bring to a simmer. Stir in the beef, then cover the pan and cook over low heat for 30 minutes.

Add the beans, lime juice, chocolate, coriander and 500 ml (17 fl oz/2 cups) water. Cover and continue to cook for a further 1½ hours, stirring occasionally, and adding more water if necessary. The consistency should be thick but not too dry. Season to taste with salt and pepper.

Serve topped with tomato, avocado and extra coriander leaves, with a side of cooked white rice.

Remember that episode of THE SIMPSONS where Homer eats that ridiculous chilli and goes on a spiritual quest, and Johnny Cash does the voice for a Space Coyote character? Well that has nothing to do with this recipe but would make for a good watch right about now.

GRILLED BUTTERMILK CHICKEN

SERVES 4

Prepare to get your hands dirty, and your hangover sated.
This messy one lends itself to a grill (broiler) or a barbecue.

INGREDIENTS

500 ml (17 fl oz/2 cups) buttermilk
4 garlic cloves, crushed
2 teaspoons wholegrain mustard
2 teaspoons hot paprika
3 teaspoons sea salt flakes
1 teaspoon freshly ground black
    pepper
2 rosemary sprigs, leaves roughly
    chopped
1.4 kg (3 lb 1 oz) whole chicken,
    cut into quarters
lemon halves, to serve

METHOD

Combine the buttermilk, garlic, mustard, paprika, salt, pepper and rosemary in a bowl.

Place the chicken in a large zip-lock bag and pour in the buttermilk mixture. Ensure the chicken pieces are well coated. Refrigerate for at least 4 hours (but ideally overnight), turning the bag occasionally to disperse the marinade.

Preheat a hooded barbecue grill to medium and lightly grease with oil. Alternatively, preheat a grill (broiler) to medium.

Remove the chicken from the marinade and drain. Place the chicken on the grill, skin side down, cover and cook for 20 minutes, turning once after 10 minutes. Turn again and cook for a further 5–10 minutes until the chicken is cooked through.

Serve with lemon halves to squeeze over the chicken.

SALTY TART

SERVES 2

*Today, sodium is your friend.
In the long run... maybe not so much.*

INGREDIENTS

2 tablespoons olive oil (or oil from the anchovy fillets, below)

5 onions, halved and thinly sliced

1 thyme sprig

1 parsley sprig

1 bay leaf

2 garlic cloves, peeled and bruised, but left whole

1 tablespoon capers, drained and rinsed

50 g (1¾ oz) good-quality anchovy fillets (about 20), drained

12 pitted black olives

1 sheet frozen puff pastry, thawed

METHOD

Firstly, caramelise the onion. Heat the olive oil in a large heavy-based frying pan over medium–low heat. Add the onion, thyme, parsley, bay leaf and garlic. Cook, stirring often, for 50–60 minutes, or until the onion is meltingly soft and slightly golden. Remove and discard the herbs and garlic.

Chop the capers and six of the anchovy fillets together. Mix them into the caramelised onion and season generously with pepper, and a little salt if required. Set aside until needed.

Preheat the oven to 200°C/400°F (fan-forced).

Place the thawed pastry sheet on a large baking tray lined with baking paper.

Gently spread the onion mixture over the pastry, leaving a 1.5 cm (½ inch) border around the edge. Bake for 20 minutes, or until the pastry is golden.

Remove from the oven and top with the remaining anchovy fillets and the olives. Bake for a further 5 minutes, or until the pastry base is crisp.

BACON & BEANS

SERVES 4

Hearty and bacony. Rich with a tiny hint of sweetness. Beany. This is comfort food at its most comfortable.

INGREDIENTS

280 g (10 oz) bacon, chopped
1 onion, finely chopped
1 garlic clove, finely chopped
½ teaspoon smoked paprika
2 x 420 g (150 oz) cans red kidney
    beans or cannellini (lima beans),
    drained
70 g (2½ oz/¼ cup) tomato paste
    (concentrated purée)
55 g (2 oz/¼ cup) soft brown sugar
2 tablespoons molasses
2 teaspoons worcestershire sauce
1 litre (34 fl oz/4 cups) vegetable stock
toasted sourdough, to serve
parsley leaves, roughly chopped,
    to serve

METHOD

Cook the bacon in a large non-stick saucepan over medium heat for 6–8 minutes, until browned. Add the onion and cook for 10 minutes over low heat, until soft. Add the garlic and paprika and cook for 1 minute until fragrant. Stir in the two cans of drained beans, tomato paste, sugar, molasses, worcestershire sauce and stock. Increase the heat, cover and bring to the boil. Reduce the heat to low again and simmer for 1 hour, stirring occasionally.

Remove the lid and simmer for a further 15 minutes, or until the sauce has thickened.

Serve the beans alongside the sourdough with parsley sprinkled over the top.

POST-LIT-SCHNIT

SERVES 4

Although often mistaken as a German invention, good ol' Wienerschnitzel was born in Vienna, Austria. We know the Austrians love schnapps, so this crumbed beauty is a classic trick to soak everything up from a tender tummy.

INGREDIENTS

50 g (1¾ oz/⅓ cup) plain (all-purpose) flour
2 free-range eggs
140 g (5 oz) panko breadcrumbs
2 tablespoons finely chopped parsley
4 veal cutlets (about 80 g/2¾ oz each)
1 onion, halved
30 g (1 oz) unsalted butter
2 tablespoons olive oil
caperberries, to serve
lemon cheeks, to serve

METHOD

Place the flour, a generous pinch of salt and pepper in a zip-lock bag. Shake the bag to combine. Whisk the eggs in a shallow bowl and combine the breadcrumbs and parsley in another shallow bowl.

Working with one cutlet at a time, place the veal between two sheets of non-stick baking paper. Use a meat mallet or rolling pin to pound the meat gently until it is about 5 mm (¼ in) thick. Rub both sides with the cut side of the onion, then repeat with the remaining pieces of veal.

Add the veal, one piece at a time, to the zip-lock bag and shake to coat in the flour mixture. Shake off the excess flour, then dip in the egg, allowing any excess liquid to drip off, and finally press into the breadcrumbs. Repeat this process with the remaining veal, then cover and refrigerate for 30 minutes.

Heat the butter and oil in a large, heavy-based frying pan until bubbling. Cook the schnitzels, in batches if necessary, for 1–2 minutes on each side or until golden and just cooked through.

Serve the schnitzels with caperberries, lemon cheeks for squeezing over.

Commence
food coma →

Jägerschnitzel translates roughly as "hunter's cutlet." Jägermeister translates to a bona fide hangover.

JAGER (MEISTER) SCHNITZEL

SERVES 4

INGREDIENTS

90 g (3 oz) plain (all-purpose) flour
1 teaspoon salt
1 teaspoon freshly ground black
 pepper
1 teaspoon garlic powder
3 free-range eggs
240 g (8½ oz/3 cups) breadcrumbs
2 tablespoons parsley
4 pork cutlets (about 100 g/3½ oz
 each), placed between sheets of
 plastic wrap and tenderised with
 a meat mallet to about 1 cm
 (½ in) thick
60 ml (2 fl oz/¼ cup) vegetable oil

MUSHROOM SAUCE

20 g (¾ oz) butter
1 teaspoon olive oil
200 g (7 oz) bacon, sliced into batons
½ small onion, finely chopped
1 garlic clove, crushed
200 g (7 oz) button mushrooms, sliced
2 tablespoons plain (all-purpose) flour
125 ml (4 fl oz/½ cup) red wine
375 ml (12½ fl oz/1½ cups) beef stock
125 ml (4 fl oz/½ cup) thick (double/
 heavy) cream

METHOD

Place the flour, salt, pepper and garlic powder in a zip-lock bag. Shake the bag to combine. Whisk the eggs in a shallow bowl and combine the breadcrumbs and parsley in another shallow bowl.

Add the pork, one cutlet at a time, to the zip-lock bag and shake to coat in the flour mixture. Shake off the excess flour, then dip in the egg, allowing any excess liquid to drip off, and finally press into the breadcrumb mixture. Repeat this process with the remaining pork cutlets, then cover and refrigerate for 30 minutes.

To make the sauce, heat the butter and olive oil in a frying pan over high heat and add the bacon. Cook until crisp, then remove with a slotted spoon and set aside to drain on paper towel. Remove all but 1 tablespoon of fat from the pan, then reduce the heat to medium and add the onion, garlic and mushrooms. Fry for 3–4 minutes, stirring occasionally, until softened. Return half the bacon to the pan and add the flour. Cook for 1–2 minutes, then add the red wine. Cook for 2–3 minutes, until the wine has reduced by one–third, then add the stock. Continue to reduce the sauce for a further 5–7 minutes, until again reduced by one–third. Finally, add the cream and cook for 5 minutes, or until the sauce has thickened.

Heat the vegetable oil in a frying pan over medium heat and add 2 cutlets. Cook for 4–5 minutes on each side, then remove from the pan and drain on paper towel. Repeat with the remaining cutlets.

Serve each cutlet with a large spoonful of sauce poured over the top. Garnish with the remaining bacon.

CHAPTER 2: THIS'LL BE A LONG DAY

You can probably make it to work on time, sure.

But come on, will they even want you there?

Sometimes there simply aren't enough breath mints
to mask the hangover halitosis.

This could be one of those times.

THE BEST BLT

SERVES 1

The BLT is the sacred union of Bacon, Lettuce and Tomato. This one has optional cheese and avocado which technically makes it a BLCAT or a BCATL or a BLACT or whatever — there's no good option here so we'll agree this is why it isn't a thing.

INGREDIENTS

4 rindless streaky bacon slices
2 slices bread
mayonnaise
lettuce leaves
½ avocado, sliced or mashed
  (optional)
4 thin slices tomato
1 slice Swiss cheese (optional)

NOTE
Why not put your hangover to the test and make some kind of fancy arrangement for your bacon? If you can assemble this sandwich, just think of what else you might be able to achieve today!

METHOD

Put the bacon in a large heavy-based frying pan and place over medium–high heat. Cook for about 3 minutes on each side until very crisp. Drain on paper towel.

Spread the bread with mayonnaise. Top with lettuce, avocado (if you're going there) and tomato, season with salt and pepper, then top with the cheese (you know you want it), bacon and the other slice of bread. Serve immediately.

Forgive me bacon, for I have sinned

These **adorable**, airy little guys are an ideal snack for a tender **tummy**. These **tasty snacks** have no relation to Sean John Combs or any other rapper/R&B artist.

CHEESE PUFF DIDDYS

MAKES 15

INGREDIENTS

40 g (1½ oz) butter
75 g (2¾ oz/½ cup) plain (all-purpose) flour
pinch of smoked paprika
¼ teaspoon sea salt
2 extra-large free-range eggs
60 g (2 oz/½ cup) grated cheddar
60 g (2 oz/½ cup) grated gruyere

NOTE
If you are a real visionary, you can easily make the puffs ahead of time, freeze the unbaked dough when you have piped or spooned it onto the baking trays. On a hungover morning, remove from the freezer and bake as directed.

METHOD

Preheat the oven to 180°C/350°F (fan-forced). Line two baking trays with baking paper.

Place the butter and 125 ml (4 fl oz/½ cup) water in a small heavy-based saucepan over medium heat. Bring to the boil, add the flour, paprika and salt and stir with a wooden spoon for 1–2 minutes, until the mixture leaves the side of the pan and forms a ball.

Transfer the mixture to the bowl of an electric mixer and allow to cool for 2 minutes. Add the eggs one at a time, beating well between each addition.

Combine the two cheeses and add three-quarters of the mixture to the bowl, stirring through until combined. The finished pastry should be firm and glossy.

Spoon the mixture into a piping (icing) bag, then pipe table-spoon sized balls of the mixture onto the lined baking trays (or just use a tablespoon), allowing space in between for rising. Sprinkle with the remaining cheese mixture and bake for 10 minutes.

Reduce the oven temperature to 160°C (320°F) and cook the puffs for a further 15 minutes, or until golden and hollow. Cool slightly on the trays.

The puffs are best gobbled down on the same day, but can be baked the day before, stored in the fridge and brought to room temperature for serving.

EGG & HAM BAGGIE

SERVES 3-4

A crusty baguette for an even crustier human.

INGREDIENTS

- 1 teaspoon white vinegar
- 6 free-range eggs
- 3 tablespoons good-quality mayonnaise
- 2 tablespoons wholegrain mustard
- 3 tablespoons chopped chives
- 4 cornichons, finely chopped
- 1 long baguette
- 160 g (5½ oz) sliced leg ham
- 2 large handfuls picked watercress (optional)

METHOD

Bring a small saucepan of water to the boil and add the vinegar. Gently lower the eggs into the boiling water and simmer for 8 minutes. Remove the eggs from the pan with a slotted spoon and refresh in cold water until cool enough to handle.

Peel the eggs and place in a bowl. Mash with a fork until roughly broken up. Add the mayonnaise, mustard, chives and cornichons and gently stir until just combined. Season with salt and pepper.

Using a large serrated knife, cut the baguette in half lengthways, leaving the back edge of the crust intact. Spread the egg mixture over the base of the baguette, then top with the ham and watercress (if using).

Close the baguette and cut into three or four portions.

Carbs

BACON CARBONARA

SERVES 4

I could eat this for breakfast, lunch and dinner. When I've been told that breakfast pasta isn't a thing, do you know what I say? "Shut up Donny, I'm hungover, and you're not my real Dad."

INGREDIENTS

400 g (14 oz) spaghetti
250 g (9 oz) bacon, chopped
1 large garlic clove, finely chopped
4 egg yolks
125 ml (4 fl oz/½ cup) thickened
    (whipping) cream (35% fat)
75 g (2¾ oz/¾ cup) finely grated
    parmesan, plus extra to serve
1 tablespoon chopped parsley

METHOD

Bring a large saucepan of salted water to the boil. Cook the spaghetti according to the packet instructions. Drain, reserving some of the cooking water.

Meanwhile, cook the bacon in a large non-stick frying pan over medium–high heat for 6–8 minutes until browned and slightly crisp. Add the garlic and cook for a further 1 minute or until fragrant.

Combine the egg yolks, cream and parmesan in a bowl. Season with salt and pepper.

Return the spaghetti to the saucepan with a tablespoon or two of the cooking water. Add the bacon and garlic to the pan. Mix the egg mixture through until well coated and creamy. Stir in the parsley.

Serve with extra parmesan cheese sprinkled over the top.

BANGERS & MASH

SERVES 4

Last night you danced to bangers then crashed.
So today...well, you get the joke.

INGREDIENTS

600 g (1 lb 5 oz) thick pork sausages
2 tablespoons peanut (ground nut) oil
2 onions, thinly sliced
2 tablespoons all-purpose curry
    powder
400 g (14 oz) tin diced tomatoes
250 ml (8½ fl oz/1 cup) beef stock
1 teaspoon soy or worcestershire
    sauce
130 g (4½ oz) frozen baby peas
55 g (2 oz) sultanas (golden raisins)
1 granny smith apple, cored,
    quartered and thinly sliced
mashed potato, to serve

METHOD

Place the sausages in a large saucepan and add enough cold water to cover. Bring to the boil over high heat, then reduce the heat to a simmer and cook for 2 minutes. Drain the sausages and leave to cool slightly, then thickly slice diagonally.

Heat 1 tablespoon of the oil in a large frying pan over medium heat. Add the sausage pieces and cook, stirring occasionally, for 3–4 minutes, until lightly browned. Using a slotted spoon, transfer to a plate and set aside. Add the remaining oil and the onion to the pan and cook, stirring occasionally, for 4–5 minutes, until soft. Add the curry powder and cook, stirring, for 1 minute, or until fragrant.

Return the sliced sausage to the pan, stir to coat in the curry mixture, then add the tomatoes, stock and soy or worcestershire sauce. Simmer, uncovered, for about 5 minutes, or until slightly thickened. Stir in the peas and sultanas and cook for a further 5 minutes, then stir through the apple.

Serve with mashed potato on the side.

Another Sunday, another

Mixing your drinks all night is a guaranteed hangover. Mixing mushrooms yields a much better result.

MIXED-SHROOM QUESADILLA

SERVES 4

INGREDIENTS

3 tablespoons olive oil
2 shallots, finely chopped
3 garlic cloves, finely chopped
400 g (14 oz) mixed mushrooms
(such as portobello, brown,
porcini, oyster, button), sliced
2 jalapeño chillies, finely chopped
½ teaspoon sea salt flakes
¼ teaspoon freshly ground pepper
8 small soft corn tortillas
1 cup grated cheese such as queso
fresco, mozzarella, fontina or
parmesan
⅓ cup coriander (cilantro) leaves,
finely chopped

METHOD

In a large mixing bowl combine 2 tablespoons of the
olive oil and the shallots, garlic, mushrooms, chillies,
salt and pepper.

Heat the remaining olive oil in a large frying pan over
medium heat. Add the mushroom mixture and cook for
5–6 minutes, until the mushrooms and shallots become
soft and begin to caramelise. Remove from the heat
and set aside to cool slightly.

Top four tortillas with the mushroom mixture. Scatter
the cheese and coriander over the top and cover with
the remaining second tortillas.

Heat a large frying pan over medium heat and cook the
quesadillas on both sides until golden brown and the
cheese is melted.

Slice each quesadilla into quarters and serve.

BURGERS

SERVES 4

A hangover tale as old as time.

INGREDIENTS

500 g (1 lb 2 oz) minced (ground)
    lean beef
1 red onion, finely chopped
½ cup parsley leaves, finely chopped
¼ cup basil leaves, finely chopped
¼ cup semi-sundried tomatoes,
    finely chopped
1 egg
½ teaspoon sea salt flakes
¼ teaspoon ground black pepper
¼ teaspoon sweet paprika
4 slices gruyere or other melty cheese
4 round bread rolls, split open
ketchup, mustard, mayonnaise, relish
    and/or chilli sauce, to serve
iceberg lettuce leaves, to serve
2 pickles, sliced
1 large tomato, sliced

METHOD

Combine the beef, onion, parsley, basil, sundried tomato, egg, salt, pepper and paprika in a large bowl. Mix well by hand. Divide into four even portions and, with wet hands, press into flat patties slightly wider than your bread rolls. Transfer to a plate, cover with plastic wrap and rest in the fridge for 30 minutes.

Heat a barbecue hotplate (griddle) or grill to medium and lightly grease with oil.

Brush or spray the burgers lightly with olive oil. Cook, turning occasionally, for 10 minutes or until cooked through. When almost cooked, top each burger with a cheese slice to melt and then toast the buns lightly on both sides.

Spread the base of each bun with your sauce/s of choice, then top with lettuce, pickle slices, the burger and tomato slices. Spread the top with any other sauce, as desired, and dig in.

GREAT MINDS DRINK ALIKE...

"Alcohol may be man's worst enemy, but the bible says love your enemy."
FRANK SINATRA

"To alcohol! The cause of, and solution to, all of life's problems."
HOMER SIMPSON

"I'd rather have a bottle in front of me than a frontal lobotomy."
DOROTHY PARKER

"There comes a time in every woman's life when the only thing that helps is a glass of champagne."
BETTE DAVIS

"When I was younger I made it a rule never to take strong drink before lunch. It is now my rule never to do so before breakfast."
WINSTON CHURCHILL

"There are two kinds of people I don't trust: people who don't drink and people who collect stickers."
CHELSEA HANDLER

The only way to improve upon potato dumplings is to shove 'em full of bacon. Duh.

BACON-STUFFED POTATO DUMPLINGS

MAKES 8 DUMPLINGS

INGREDIENTS

1 kg (2 lb 3 oz) medium-sized
    floury potatoes
1 teaspoon sea salt
90 g (3 oz/¾ cup) potato flour
    or cornflour (corn starch)
2 egg yolks
pinch of freshly grated nutmeg

FILLING

1 tablespoon olive oil
250 g (9 oz) smoked bacon,
    finely diced
1 small onion, finely chopped
1 teaspoon chopped parsley

METHOD

To make the filling, heat the oil in a frying pan over medium heat. Add the bacon and onion and cook, stirring occasionally, for 10 minutes or until the fat has rendered and the onion is golden brown. Set aside to cool a little, then combine with the parsley.

Boil the potatoes in plenty of salted boiling water for 10 minutes or until a knife slips easily through the flesh. Drain, set aside to cool a little, then peel. Press the potatoes through a potato ricer over a heatproof bowl and set aside to cool completely. Mix the potato with the salt, flour, egg yolks and nutmeg to form a dough. Evenly divide the dough and filling into eight portions. Using damp hands, roll the dough into dumplings. Press a hole into each dumpling and spoon in the filling. Reshape until smooth.

Bring a large saucepan of salted water to a simmering boil over medium heat. Add the dumplings, in batches if necessary, and cook for 15–20 minutes, until the dumplings rise to the top of the pan – take care that the water does not boil, as the dumplings will disintegrate.

BACON-WRAPPED STUFFED ONIONS

MAKES 6

INGREDIENTS

6 small–medium onions, ends trimmed and inner layers hollowed out (reserve and finely chop inner layers)
1 tablespoon olive oil
2 pork sausages, removed from their casings and chopped
1 celery stalk, thinly sliced
1½ teaspoons thyme leaves
1½ teaspoons chopped sage
100 g (3½ oz/1¼ cups) fresh breadcrumbs
20 g (¾ oz) butter, melted
80 ml (2½ fl oz/⅓ cup) chicken stock
6 slices streaky bacon

METHOD

Preheat the oven to 180°C/350°F (fan-forced).

Place the hollowed-out onions in a bowl of cold water and leave to soak while you make the stuffing.

Heat the olive oil in a frying pan over medium heat and fry the sausage meat until cooked through, mashing with a wooden spoon as it cooks to ensure there are no large pieces of meat. Remove from the pan with a slotted spoon, into a bowl.

Add the reserved chopped onion and the celery to the pan. Reduce the heat to medium–low and cook for 4–5 minutes, or until softened, but not browned.

Add the onion and celery to the sausage meat, along with the herbs and breadcrumbs. Season well with salt and pepper. Add the melted butter and stock, then stir to combine.

Drain the onions. Lay on a flat surface and use your hands or a small spoon to stuff each onion cavity with the sausage mixture, ensuring the stuffing is firmly packed. Wrap a slice of bacon around each onion, then secure with a toothpick.

Transfer to the oven and roast for 20 minutes, or until the bacon is golden brown.

Serve hot, removing the toothpicks just before serving.

Stuff it, wrap it, cook it,
eat it, then go back to bed.

Cheese hath become me →

BACON MAC ATTACK

SERVES 4

Don't wig out: this mac recipe uses cream instead of a béchamel sauce, so you got this!

INGREDIENTS

250 g (9 oz) macaroni
500 ml (17 fl oz/2 cups) thickened (whipping) cream (35% fat)
1 large garlic clove, smashed
1 large thyme sprig
200 g (7 oz) bacon, chopped
180 g (6½ oz/1½ cups) grated cheddar
100 g (3½ oz/1 cup) finely grated parmesan
pinch of freshly grated nutmeg
70 g (2½ oz/1 cup) fresh breadcrumbs
2 tablespoons olive oil
pinch of smoked paprika

METHOD

Bring a large saucepan of salted water to the boil. Cook the macaroni according to packet instuctions, or until al dente. Drain.

Meanwhile, preheat the oven to 180°C (350°F). Lightly grease a 1 litre (34 fl oz/4 cup) capacity baking dish.

Combine the cream, garlic and thyme in a saucepan over medium heat. Bring to a simmer, then remove from the heat and allow to infuse for a few minutes.

Cook the bacon in a non-stick frying pan over medium–high heat for 6–8 minutes until slightly browned and crisp.

Strain the solids from the cream mixture. Strip the thyme leaves and return to the cream, discarding the stalk. Add 1 cup of the cheddar and all of the parmesan and nutmeg and stir until the cheeses have melted. Season with salt and pepper. Add the macaroni and bacon to the cream mixture and stir until well coated. Pour into the prepared dish.

Combine the breadcrumbs, remaining cheddar and the oil in a bowl and sprinkle over the top of the macaroni. Sprinkle with a little smoked paprika. Bake for 10 minutes until golden and crunchy.

(ALMOST) CHINESE TAKEOUT

SERVES 4

INGREDIENTS

¼ teaspoon bicarbonate of soda
   (baking soda)
500 g (1 lb 2 oz) skinless chicken
   breast or thigh fillets, thinly sliced
1 tablespoon soy sauce
60 ml (2 fl oz/¼ cup) Shaoxing
   rice wine
5 teaspoons cornflour (corn starch)
1 tablespoon brown sugar
1 tablespoon all-purpose curry
   powder
1 teaspoon Chinese five-spice
180 ml (6 fl oz) chicken stock
2–3 tablespoons peanut (ground nut)
   or vegetable oil
1 onion, cut into thick wedges
1 red capsicum (bell pepper), cut into
   2.5 cm (1 in) diamonds
1 head broccoli, cut into florets and
   steamed for 2 minutes
2 garlic cloves, crushed
2 cm (¾ in) piece ginger, grated
steamed rice, to serve
prawn crackers, to serve

METHOD

Combine the bicarbonate of soda with 1 tablespoon
water in a medium bowl. Add the chicken and toss to
coat. Set aside at room temperature for 5 minutes.

Whisk the soy sauce, 1 tablespoon of the rice wine,
2 teaspoons of the cornflour and 1 teaspoon of the
sugar in a small bowl. Add to the chicken mixture,
stir to coat, and marinate for 15–20 minutes.

Whisk the remaining rice wine, cornflour and sugar
together in a bowl with the curry powder, five-spice
and stock. Set aside.

Heat a small splash of the oil in a large wok or
deep frying pan over high heat until very hot and
just smoking. Add half the chicken and stir-fry for
3 minutes, or until lightly browned all over and just
cooked through. Transfer to a plate. Repeat with a little
more oil and the remaining chicken.

Return the wok or frying pan to high heat, add a little
more oil and heat until the oil begins to smoke. Add
the onion, capsicum and steamed broccoli and cook,
stirring occasionally, for about 4 minutes, until the
vegetables are browned in spots and tender-crisp.
Return the chicken and any juices to the wok or
pan and add the garlic and ginger. Stir-fry for about
1 minute, or until fragrant.

Whisk the reserved sauce again to combine, then add
to the wok or pan and cook, stirring constantly, for
1 minute, or until the sauce thickens.

Serve with steamed rice and prawn crackers.

Admittedly this is **harder** than getting Chinese takeout, but you've already made it to page 60. **So just cook it.**

MERCIFUL CHIPOTLE NACHOS

SERVES 4

Hangover got you feeling strung out?
The answer is stringy cheese, my friend.

INGREDIENTS

1 tablespoon vegetable oil
1 onion, chopped
3 tablespoons tomato paste
     (concentrated purée)
2 teaspoons ground cumin
2 garlic cloves, crushed
500 g (1 lb 2 oz) minced (ground) beef
300 g (10½ oz) tinned kidney beans,
     drained
250 ml (8½ fl oz/1 cup) beer
2 chipotle chillies in adobo sauce,
     chopped, plus 2 teaspoons of the
     adobo sauce
large handful of coriander (cilantro),
     including the stalks and leaves,
     chopped
250 g (9 oz) tortilla chips
250 g (9 oz/2 cups) grated mature
     cheddar
shredded lettuce, to serve
200 g (7 oz) cherry tomatoes, halved
1 avocado, chopped
sour cream to serve (optional)
sliced pickled jalapeños, to serve

METHOD

Heat the oil in a frying pan over medium–low heat and cook the onion, stirring often, for 5–6 minutes, or until softened. Add the tomato paste, cumin and garlic and cook, stirring, for 2 minutes.

Increase the heat to medium–high and add the beef. Cook, stirring, for 6–8 minutes, or until the beef changes colour. Stir in the kidney beans, beer, chopped chipotle chillies, adobo sauce and chopped coriander stalks. Bring to the boil, then reduce the heat and simmer, uncovered, for about 15 minutes, or until the liquid is almost evaporated and the mixture has thickened. Stir in the coriander leaves and season to taste with salt and pepper.

Preheat the oven to 170°C (340°F). Spread half the tortilla chips over the base of a baking tray or baking dish suitable for serving. Scatter with half the cheese and top with a little less than half the beef mixture.

Repeat with a second layer of tortilla chips, most of the cheese (reserve some for the top), the remaining beef and then the remaining cheese.

Bake for 5 minutes, or until the tortilla chips are lightly toasted and the cheese is melted.

Top with the lettuce, tomato, avocado, sour cream and jalapeño chilli. Serve immediately.

WAFFLE NACHOS

SERVES 4

INGREDIENTS

1 tablespoon vegetable oil
1 chorizo sausage, about 100 g
    (3½ oz), sliced
250 g (9 oz) packet of English-style
    waffles
coriander (cilantro), for garnish

CREAMY CORN CHEESE

250 g (9 oz/2 cups) grated mature
    cheddar
2 × 125 g (4½ oz) cans creamed corn
60 g (2 oz/¼ cup) good-quality
    mayonnaise
¼ small onion, finely chopped

SPICY BLACK BEANS

1 tablespoon olive oil
1 red onion, finely chopped
2 garlic cloves, crushed
400 g (14 oz) tin black beans, drained
1 tablespoon roughly chopped pickled
    jalapeño chilli
1 teaspoon ground cumin
handful of coriander (cilantro),
    chopped

METHOD

Combine the creamy corn cheese ingredients in
a bowl. Season to taste with salt and pepper.

For the beans, heat the oil in a frying pan over
medium–low heat and cook the onion and garlic,
stirring occasionally, for 6–8 minutes, or until
tender. Add the beans, chilli, cumin and 80 ml
(2½ fl oz/⅓ cup) water. Cook, stirring and mashing
some of the beans, for 6–8 minutes, or until most of
the liquid has evaporated. Stir in the coriander, then
season to taste.

Preheat the oven to 170°C (340°F).

Heat the oil in a frying pan over medium–low heat.
Cook the chorizo for 5–6 minutes, or until browned
and a little crispy around the edges. Remove from the
pan using a slotted spoon and drain on paper towel.

Meanwhile, heat the waffles according to the packet
instructions, then cut in half on the diagonal.

Spread half the waffles over the base of a baking tray
or baking dish suitable for serving. Spoon a little less
than half the beans and half the creamy corn cheese
over the top. Repeat with a second layer of waffles,
then the remaining beans and creamy corn cheese.
Bake for 6–8 minutes, or until the cheese in the
topping is melted.

Top with the chorizo, scatter with coriander and
serve immediately.

It's the freak mutation
of nachos you didn't
even know you needed,
till this very moment.
Prepare thyself.

This'll help,
or perhaps
kill you.

CHERRY CHOC PIZZA

SERVES 6

Three simple words.
Eat. Dessert. Pizza.

INGREDIENTS

olive oil, for greasing
50 g (1¾ oz) mascarpone
2 teaspoons soft brown sugar
1 plain frozen pizza base, thawed
zest of ½ lemon
2 cups cherries, pitted
shaved dark chocolate, for topping
1 tablespoon of salt flakes
mint leaves, to garnish

METHOD

Preheat the oven to 200°C/400°F. Line a large baking tray with baking paper and lightly grease with oil.

In a small bowl, combine the mascarpone, brown sugar and lemon zest, then spread the mixture over the thawed pizza base. Arrange the cherries evenly over the top, lightly pressing into the dough.

Place the tray in the oven, cover and cook for 15–20 minutes until the base is well cooked.

Remove from the heat and scatter with chocolate, sprinkle with salt flakes and garnish with the mint leaves. Slice and serve.

CHAPTER 3:
BEDRIDDEN & BROKEN

Not a chance you're leaving the house today.

Luckily for you, the recipes in this chapter

are specifically designed to be eaten while

softly weeping on the couch and

half-watching Netflix.

FANCY TUNA MELT

SERVES 2

INGREDIENTS

180 g (6½ oz) tinned tuna
¼ red onion, finely chopped
1 small celery stalk, thinly sliced
2 tablespoons sweetcorn kernels
1 tablespoon good-quality mayonnaise
2 thick slices white or wholemeal
    (whole-wheat) bread
4 slices jarlsberg or similar cheese

METHOD

Flake the tuna into a small bowl and add the red onion, celery and sweetcorn. Season with a pinch of salt and lots of black pepper, then mix in the mayonnaise.

Preheat the grill (broiler) to high. Lightly toast the bread on both sides.

Spoon the tuna mixture onto the bread and place the cheese on top. Grill for 2–3 minutes until the cheese is melted and bubbling.

High in protein and low in effort: this is what your brain and body need right now.

MORE ↗
CARBS

CROQUE MONSIEUR

MAKES 4

Want to French-up your hangover?
Have we got the guy for you!

INGREDIENTS

8 slices good-quality sourdough
    bread
40 g (1½ oz) butter, softened
3 tablespoons dijon mustard
200 g (7 oz) good-quality sliced
    leg ham
60 g (2 oz/½ cup) grated gruyère

BECHAMEL SAUCE

15 g (½ oz) butter
1 tablespoon plain (all-purpose) flour
125 ml (4 fl oz/½ cup) milk
40 g (1½ oz/⅓ cup) grated gruyère
1 tablespoon finely chopped parsley
white pepper, to taste

METHOD

To make the béchamel sauce, melt the butter in a small heavy-based saucepan over medium heat. Add the flour and stir to make a smooth paste. Cook, stirring, for 1 minute, or until bubbling, then gradually whisk in the milk until smooth. Simmer for a further 1–2 minutes, until thick.

Remove from the heat and stir in the gruyère until melted. Add the parsley, stir and season lightly with salt and white pepper. Press a piece of baking paper over the surface of the sauce to stop a skin forming, then set aside.

Generously spread one side of each slice of bread with the butter; spread the other side with the mustard. Place four of the buttered slices in a large heavy-based frying pan, buttered side down, and top with the ham. Carefully spread the béchamel sauce over, then sprinkle with the gruyere. Finish with the remaining bread, butter side up.

Place the pan over medium–low heat and cook the sandwiches, turning occasionally, for about 15 minutes, or until the bread is deep golden and very crispy, and the cheese inside has melted.

Transfer from the frying pan to a wire rack to cool for about 3 minutes, and enjoy.

GRILLED TRIPLE CHEESE

SERVES 2

INGREDIENTS

50 g (1¾ oz) gruyère, grated
50 g (1¾ oz) red Leicester, grated
50 g (1¾ oz) cheddar, grated
butter, for spreading
4 slices white or wholemeal
    (whole-wheat) sandwich bread

METHOD

Combine the grated cheeses in a small bowl and season with a pinch of salt and a good grind of pepper.

Heat a sandwich toaster/jaffle iron. Generously butter the bread on one side.

Sprinkle the cheese on the unbuttered side of two bread slices and place the remaining bread on top, butter side up.

Transfer to the preheated sandwich toaster and toast for 4–5 minutes until golden brown and the cheese is starting to ooze out the sides. Don't toast for any longer or the cheese will quickly melt through the bread leaving you with soggy bread devoid of filling, which would be very sad and only worsen your hungover mood.

Why have one cheese, when you can have **THREE?**

If you need me,
I'll be on the
couch, forever

STUFFED SANDWICH

SERVES 4-6

Behold: the densest sandwich
in recorded human history.

INGREDIENTS

1 x 20 cm (8 inch) round rustic
    bread loaf
2 tablespoons olive oil
2 teaspoons apple cider vinegar
2 anchovy fillets, chopped
½ small red onion, finely chopped
2 free-range eggs, hard-boiled,
    peeled and sliced
180 g (6½ oz) tinned tuna in
    olive oil, drained
40 g (1½ oz/⅓ cup) pitted black
    olives, roughly chopped
1 red capsicum (bell pepper),
    thinly sliced
2 tomatoes, thickly sliced
1 Lebanese (short) cucumber,
    thinly sliced

METHOD

Use a serrated knife to cut the loaf horizontally, all the way through; it helps to make the base larger than the top. Remove a little of the inside of the bread, to create a cavity. Sprinkle both cut sides of the loaf with the olive oil and vinegar.

Scatter the anchovy evenly over the base of the loaf, then top with the onion and egg slices.

In a small bowl, break up the tuna chunks with a fork. Add the olives and capsicum and stir to combine. Spread the tuna mixture over the egg slices. Lay the tomato over the top and sprinkle with salt and pepper. Add the cucumber, then place the bread lid on top.

Firmly press the loaf back together again, then wrap tightly with plastic wrap. Place on a tray or cutting board, and place another tray or board on top and press down for a few minutes, or place some tins of food on top to compress the loaf.

Refrigerate for at least 4 hours. Unwrap and slice into wedges and serve.

THE ELVIS

SERVES 2

INGREDIENTS

4 slices bacon
2 tablespoons maple syrup, plus extra
    to serve (optional)
80 g (2¾ oz) peanut butter
4 slices white or wholemeal
    (whole-wheat) sandwich bread
2 bananas, thinly sliced
knob of butter

METHOD

Preheat the oven to 180°C (350°F). Place the bacon on a wire rack over a roasting tin, then roast for 15 minutes, until browned but not crisp.

Carefully remove from the oven and brush the bacon all over with the maple syrup, ensuring that each side is well coated. Return to the oven for 5 minutes, then set aside to cool.

To assemble, spread 1 tablespoon of peanut butter on each slice of bread. Layer two of the slices with the banana and the other two slices with bacon, then smush the two halves together.

Melt the butter in a non-stick frying pan over medium heat.

Add the sandwiches and fry for 3–4 minutes on each side, until golden brown.

Drizzle with extra maple syrup if using, and serve immediately, remembering that the contents will be super hot!

Any sandwich that was good enough for **The King** himself, is honestly probably too good for you right now.

Merci beaucoup for French fries

BACON & FRENCH FRY SANDWICH

SERVES 2

INGREDIENTS

4 slices bacon
butter, for spreading
4 thick slices white bread
a few handfuls of takeout French fries
    (hot chips)
brown sauce or tomato ketchup

METHOD

Heat 1 teaspoon of oil in a frying pan over medium heat and add the bacon. Cook until crisp or cooked to your liking.

Butter the bread and divide the bacon and fries between the sandwiches. Top with brown sauce or tomato ketchup, or both.

23-AND-A-HALF EXCUSES TO GET OUTTA WORK

"Sorry Greg, I've come down with a touch of the bubonic plague."

"Sorry Greg, my florist is giving birth and I need to be there to film."

"Sorry Greg, my dentist said that typing will be bad for my cavities."

"Sorry Greg, I've been chosen last minute to audition for the circus. Yes, it's always been my dream!"

"Sorry Greg, my bike was stolen from the pub last ni— I mean, my bike was stolen."

"Sorry Greg, Esmerelda, my psychic and spiritual counsel, has advised me to spend today working on my relationship with my cat."

"Sorry Greg, I was up all night reading existentialist prose and I'm just feeling a bit too aware of the pointlessness of my existence this morning to come into work."

"Sorry Greg, I'm being flown to L.A. to receive my star on the Walk Of Fame. Very last minute, yes..."

"Sorry Greg, my train conductor has gone on strike."

"Sorry Greg, my neighbour's cat is lonely."

"Morning Greg! I was just calling to (play very loud audio of screeching bus tyres near your phone microphone)..."

"Sorry Greg, I'm being flown to Stockholm to accept the Nobel Prize for life achievements in office administration."

"Sorry Greg, Mercury is in retrograde and you know how that affects my ability to perform at work."

"Greg, we discussed this? I asked for the day off six months ago."

"Sorry Greg, I'd like to plead the fifth."

"Sorry Greg, Mother and I are starting an acroyoga accreditation course today."

"Sorry Greg, I've had a temporary psychotic break with reality."

"Sorry Greg, there's been a hyperlocal earthquake just near my train station, and everything is out of action."

"Sorry Greg, you know how upsetting last night's BRITISH BAKE OFF results were."

"Sorry Greg, I'm actually calling from an alien spacecraft and they're going to need me for probing purposes all day."

"Sorry Greg, I'm really close to cracking the high score here and I simply can't close the game."

"Sorry Greg, I've decided that the role isn't satisfying me professionally and I just feel as though I need a day to really think about my place in, and future with, the company."

"Sorry Greg, I think the work email server has become sentient and thirsts for my flesh and blood. I'd rather steer clear of that today."

23-and-a-half: "Sorry Greg, too hungover. See you tomorrow."

FRENCH FRY CURRY

SERVES 4

How many cookbooks ask you to run out to the nearest shop for some takeout fries? Not enough.

INGREDIENTS

1 tablespoon butter
1 tablespoon peanut (ground nut) oil
2 onions, finely chopped
2 garlic cloves, crushed
1 tablespoon tomato paste
   (concentrated purée)
2 tablespoons plain (all-purpose) flour
1 tablespoon all-purpose curry
   powder, or to taste (use a hot
   curry powder if you prefer a
   spicier curry sauce)
1 teaspoon sweet paprika
375 ml (12½ fl oz/1½ cups) chicken
   or vegetable stock
½ teaspoon soy sauce
squeeze of lemon juice, to taste
LOTS of takeout french fries
   (hot chips)

METHOD

Heat the butter and oil in a medium saucepan over low heat. Add the onion and garlic and cook, stirring frequently, for 6–8 minutes, until softened. Add the tomato paste and cook, stirring, for 1 minute, then stir in the flour, curry powder and paprika. Cook, stirring constantly, for 1–2 minutes, until the mixture starts to stick on the base of the pan. Remove the pan from the heat and gradually whisk in the stock until smooth. Return the pan to medium heat, bring to the boil, stirring often, then reduce the heat to low and simmer, stirring occasionally, for 8–10 minutes, until thickened.

Blitz with a hand-held blender for a smooth sauce or just blend it a little, to leave some texture. Stir in the soy sauce, a squeeze of lemon juice to taste and add a little salt if necessary. Add a little boiling water to thin the consistency if you prefer a thinner sauce.

To serve, spread fries on a plate and spoon the sauce over the top.

Sobriety, I hardly knew thee

How many potatoes must I eat before I, too, am a potato?

BAKED POTATO... THINGS

SERVES 2

*You don't need to leave the house to see the light today.
Just bake these carb-tastic... things.*

INGREDIENTS

8 medium-sized roasting potatoes
60 g (2 oz) butter
2 tablespoons olive oil
1 teaspoon thyme leaves, plus extra
    to garnish
1 teaspoon chopped rosemary leaves
1 teaspoon sumac

METHOD

Preheat the oven to 180°C/350°F (fan-forced). Line a baking tray with foil.

Cut thin slices into each potato, but don't cut all the way down to the bottom. Place on the baking tray.

Melt about 1 tablespoon of the butter, and mix with the olive oil, thyme, rosemary and sumac. Brush the butter mixture onto the potatoes, using the bristles to gently get some of the butter between the slices. Season with salt and pepper.

Transfer to the oven and roast for 30 minutes. Melt the remaining butter, use it to baste the potatoes, then roast for a further 15 minutes.

Season with salt and pepper, garnish with extra thyme and serve.

POTATO CRISP & BACON NACHOS

SERVES 4

INGREDIENTS

1 tablespoon vegetable oil
6 bacon slices, cut into thin strips
250 g (9 oz) plain crinkle-cut potato
  crisps
185 g (6½ oz/1½ cups) grated mature
  cheddar
150 g (5½ oz/1 cup) grated mozzarella
Guacamole (page 109), to serve
  (optional)
sour cream, to serve (optional)
1 spring onion (scallion), thinly sliced

METHOD

Preheat the oven to 170°C (340°F).

Heat the oil in a frying pan over medium–high heat. Add the bacon and cook, stirring occasionally, for 5–6 minutes until crispy. Drain on paper towel.

Spread half the crisps over the base of a baking tray or baking dish suitable for serving. Combine the cheeses and scatter half over the crisps, followed by just less than half the bacon. Add layers of the remaining crisps, the remaining cheese and remaining bacon.

Bake for 5 minutes, or until the crisps are lightly toasted and the cheese is melted.

Top with the guacamole and sour cream, if using, or serve it on the side. Scatter with the spring onion and serve.

Absolutely tragic? Yes.
The highlight of your day,
month and year?
Also, yes.

GERMAN POTATO CAKES

MAKES 8

Danke to our German brothers and sisters for creating the Kartoffelpuffer. This hearty street food staple is perfect for soaking up some Oktoberfest shenanigans.

INGREDIENTS

450 g (1 lb) medium potatoes, peeled and grated
2 small onions, grated
¼ teaspoon salt
75 g (2¾ oz/½ cup) plain (all-purpose) flour
2 free-range eggs, lightly beaten
125 ml (4 fl oz/½ cup) vegetable oil
apple sauce, to serve
mint leaves, to garnish

METHOD

Combine the potato, onion, salt and flour in a bowl. Add the egg and mix well.

Heat the oil in a large frying pan over medium–high heat.

Fill a ⅓ cup with the potato mixture and place the mixture in the pan. Flatten with the back of a spatula until the fritter is about 1.5 cm (½ in) thick. Repeat this process, until you have 3–4 fritters in the pan. Fry for 3–4 minutes on each side, until golden brown and cooked through. Transfer to paper towel to drain, then repeat with the remaining mixture.

Serve the fritters with warm or cold apple sauce and garnish with mint leaves.

GARLICKY TOMATO TART

SERVES 4

INGREDIENTS

3 whole garlic bulbs, unpeeled
olive oil, for drizzling
1 sheet frozen puff pastry, thawed
milk, for brushing
200 g (7 oz) good-quality ricotta
zest of 1 lemon (optional)
300 g (10½ oz) cherry tomatoes,
    cut in half
small handful thyme sprigs, leaves
    picked
balsamic vinegar, for drizzling

METHOD

Preheat the oven to 160°C (320°F). Line
a baking tray with baking paper.

Slice the top one-quarter off the garlic bulbs and
discard. Place the garlic bulbs on a large square of foil
and drizzle with a little olive oil. Wrap the garlic in
the foil and roast in the oven for 40 minutes, or until
completely soft. Set aside to cool.

Trim off and reserve about 1 cm (½ inch) from each
side of the pastry. Place the pastry on the lined baking
tray. Brush the outer edges of the pastry with milk and
place the trimmed edges on top, to form a small crust
during baking.

Squeeze the roasted garlic cloves into a small bowl.
Add the ricotta and lemon zest, if using. Season
generously with salt and pepper and mix well.

Spread the ricotta mixture over the pastry, avoiding
the border around the edge. Arrange the tomatoes on
top, cut side up. Sprinkle with the thyme, drizzle with
a little more oil and season with salt and pepper.

Transfer to the oven and bake for about 30 minutes,
or until the pastry is golden brown.

Drizzle with balsamic vinegar and serve.

This crispy tart might just restart your heart.

↓

POTATO SALAD

SERVES 6

Cooking potatoes in chicken stock is about to become your new favourite hangover pastime.

INGREDIENTS

3 free-range eggs
1 teaspoon olive oil
200 g (7 oz) bacon, sliced
1 kg (2 lb 3 oz) baby potatoes
3 chicken stock cubes
½ red onion, thinly sliced
15 cornichons or small pickles,
    sliced lengthways
1 small bunch parsley, finely
    chopped
1 small bunch chives, snipped

DRESSING
125 ml (4 fl oz/½ cup) olive oil
60 ml (2 fl oz/¼ cup) white wine
    vinegar
2 tablespoons dijon mustard
pinch of sugar

METHOD

In a small bowl, whisk together all of the ingredients for the dressing, season with salt and pepper and set aside.

Place the eggs in a small saucepan, cover with cold water and bring to the boil over high heat. Reduce to a rolling simmer and cook for 6 minutes. Remove from the heat and place the eggs directly into iced water. Once cool, peel and cut in half lengthways.

Heat the olive oil in a frying pan over high heat and add the bacon. Cook until crisp, then remove with a slotted spoon and set aside to drain on paper towel.

Place the potatoes in a large saucepan, cover with water and bring to the boil. Add the stock cubes and cook for about 15 minutes, or until a knife slips through the potatoes easily. Drain, then halve or quarter the potatoes depending on their size. Transfer to a large bowl and allow to cool for a few minutes. Add the red onion, bacon, cornichons, herbs and the dressing. Toss to combine until everything is evenly coated in the dressing, then add the eggs and gently combine. Serve warm.

BACON HASH

SERVES 4

INGREDIENTS

1 kg (2 lb 3 oz) waxy potatoes,
  cut into cubes
280 g (10 oz) bacon, chopped
60 ml (2 fl oz/¼ cup) olive oil
1 red capsicum (bell pepper),
  finely chopped
2 garlic cloves, crushed
1 teaspoon smoked paprika
2 thyme sprigs
4 spring onions (scallions),
  finely chopped
4 free-range eggs

METHOD

Place the potato in a large saucepan and cover with cold water. Bring to the boil and cook the potatoes for 2 minutes, or until just tender. Drain well.

Cook the bacon in a large non-stick frying pan over medium–high heat for 8–10 minutes, until very crisp. Using a slotted spoon, transfer the bacon to a plate. Add the potatoes to the pan and cook over medium heat for 10 minutes, or until browned and crisp. Transfer to the plate with the bacon.

Add 2 tablespoons of the oil and the capsicum to the pan and cook for 2–3 minutes until the capsicum has softened. Stir in the garlic, paprika and thyme and cook for 1 minute. Return the bacon and potatoes to the pan and toss until warmed through. Season well with salt and pepper. Stir in the spring onion then transfer the mixture to a serving plate or plates.

Meanwhile, heat the remaining oil in a frying pan over medium–high heat and fry the eggs until cooked to your liking. Serve on top of the hash.

This really is the **ultimate** hangover breakfast, lunch or dinner.
Packed with carbs and salt, it's good for what ails you
and it's already in bite-sized pieces for ease of recovery.
All you need is someone else
to cook it
for you... →

BACON-Y SRIRACHA ONION RINGS

MAKES 8

A burning ring of fire might serve to distract you from the feeling that your entire world is on fire.

INGREDIENTS

4 large onions
3 tablespoons sriracha hot sauce
16 slices rindless streaky bacon, halved lengthways

METHOD

Line two large baking trays with foil and place a wire rack on top of each. (There's no need to preheat the oven for this recipe. It's better to start with a cold oven.)

Cut two 1.5 cm (½ in) wide rings from the widest part of each onion, being careful to keep the slices intact. Carefully pop out the centre two-thirds of each large ring, leaving two or three layers for each ring. You should have 8 onion rings. Save the leftover onion for another use.

Brush each onion ring with the hot sauce. Carefully wrap each coated ring with bacon, overlapping the bacon slightly as you wrap it around. You will need two strips of bacon for each ring. Secure the ends of the bacon strips with toothpicks as you go. Place the wrapped onion rings on the wire rack and place in the oven. Set the oven to 140°C (275°F) and bake for 30 minutes.

Increase the oven temperature to 160°C (320°F) and continue baking for a further 20–25 minutes until the onion is tender and the bacon is crisp.

Remove from the oven and carefully remove the toothpicks.

CHAPTER 4:
BEYOND SALVATION

Today is a dark day.
Memories of last night are darker still.

The traditional concept of a
'meal' is out of the question.

Stronger medication
is required.

CANDIED BEER BACON

MAKES 24

Sweet, sweet, bacon. For this recipe you can repurpose the half-drunk can of stout sitting on your counter. Snack on these candy bits by the fistful, or use as a garnish for your Bloody Marys (page 115).

INGREDIENTS

110 g (4 oz/½ cup) soft brown sugar
60 ml (2 fl oz/¼ cup) stout or other dark beer
2 tablespoons pure maple syrup
12 bacon slices, cut in half crossways

METHOD

Preheat the oven to 160°C (320°F). Line a large baking tray with foil and place a wire rack on top.

Whisk the sugar, beer and maple syrup together in a small bowl, until the mixture is syrupy.

Brush the the glaze on both sides of the bacon and place in a single layer on the wire rack.

Bake for 15 minutes. Remove from the oven and brush all over with more glaze. Return to the oven for a further 20–25 minutes, brushing with more glaze every 10 or so minutes, until the bacon is deeply browned and lacquered. Remove any pieces that are on the verge of burning. Keep a careful eye on it from about the 30-minute mark. It won't be totally crisp yet, but will crisp further on cooling.

Remove from the oven, cool on the rack for 5 minutes, and then transfer to a tray lined with a baking paper to cool completely.

Eat immediately.

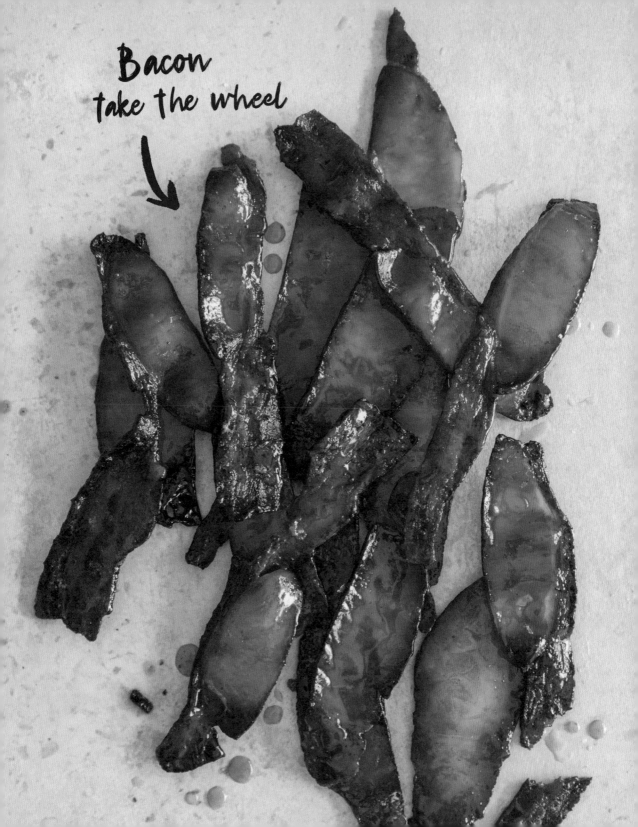

Bacon
take the wheel

Replete with sprinkles, and a sprinkling of hangover shame!

CHOC-COATED BACON

MAKES 12

INGREDIENTS

150 g (5½ oz) dark chocolate, chopped
12 slices Candied beer bacon
    (page 102)
sprinkles, to coat

NOTE
For a spicy kick to the glaze, add a splash of hot sauce, or a pinch of smoked hot paprika or cayenne pepper.

METHOD

Line a large baking tray with baking paper.

Melt two-thirds of the chocolate gently in a small heatproof bowl set over a pan of simmering water. Remove from the heat, add the remaining chocolate and stir until smooth.

Working with one bacon slice at a time, dip the bottom half of the bacon into the chocolate and allow the excess to drip off. Holding the bacon over another bowl, scatter the sprinkles over the chocolate-coated area and place onto the prepared tray. Refrigerate for 20 minutes or until set.

Store in a sealed container in the refrigerator for 1–2 days.

COB STORY

MAKES 4 COBS

Vegetables for a hangover? Yes. Don't you see...?
The corn is merely a vessel for the chipotle mayo.

INGREDIENTS

4 corn cobs, husks removed
smoked paprika, for sprinkling
¼ cup finely grated manchego
    or parmesan
1 lime, quartered, to serve

CHIPOTLE MAYO

juice of 1 lime
1 tablespoon chipotle sauce
125 g (4½ oz/½ cup) good-quality
    mayonnaise

METHOD

Heat a barbecue grill to high and lightly grease
with oil.

Blanch the corn in a large saucepan of boiling water
for 1 minute, then drain.

To make the chipotle mayo, combine the ingredients
in a small bowl, stirring to combine well.

Brush or spray the corn with olive oil and cook on the
grill, turning occasionally, for about 10 minutes or until
charred. Transfer to a serving platter.

Spread a small spoonful of chipotle mayo over each
cob. Sprinkle with smoked paprika and cheese.

Serve with any remaining chipotle mayonnaise and
with lime wedges for squeezing.

GUACAMOLE

MAKES 1½ CUPS

A classic side dish will, on this day, become your primary snack. Obviously, dollop on some fresh toasted sourdough if you're fancy like that.

INGREDIENTS

2 ripe avocados, mashed with a fork
½ fresh jalapeño chilli, seeded and finely chopped
½ small red onion, finely chopped
juice of ½ a lime, plus extra to taste
handful of coriander (cilantro) leaves, roughly chopped
tortilla chips or toasted sourdough, to serve

METHOD

Combine the avocado, chilli and onion in a bowl. Add the lime juice and season with salt, to taste.

Stir in the coriander and season with more lime juice, if you like.

THE WHAT'D I DO LAST NIGHT? QUIZ

Let's piece back together the shameful jigsaw that is your memory of last night's shenanigans. You may circle as many or as few as apply.

Q1: LAST NIGHT YOU CONSUMED:

a) A nine-course degustation you've been saving for since 2013 but recall only small fragments thereof.

b) Your bodyweight in fries.

c) A dubious burrito from a street vendor who is now texting you hourly.

d) Nothing – you drank on an empty stomach and are now struggling to live.

Q2: YOU TEXTED THE FOLLOWING:

a) A past, current or prospective employer.

b) A past, current or prospective co-worker.

c) A past, current or prospective lover.

d) Your mother.

yikes

Q3: WITH YOUR UBER DRIVER, TOPICS OF CONVERSATION INCLUDED:

a) What fine upholstery the vehicle had.

b) True crime podcasts.

c) Geopolitics.

d) Crushed hopes for the screenplay you've been developing since high school.

Oh boy

Q4: YOUR NEW TATTOO READS:

a) "I HEART BRAD"

b) "Live. Love. Laugh."

c) "Geopolitics."

d) full back tattoo of Meryl Streep's iconic role as the ruthless Miranda Priestly in **THE DEVIL WEARS PRADA**

Answers revealed

RESULTS: Tally the total number of answers you circled.

0: You do not need this book. Please try harder.

1–4: A respectable effort.

5–10: We need more people like you in this world. Want to grab another drink tonight?

10–15: Truly impressive. You should immediately consume a Post-Lit-Schnif (page 32).

16: You are concrete proof that God walks among us. But still: seek help.

DRY TOAST

SERVES 1 SAD SOUL

Judge not, lest ye be judged.

INGREDIENTS

sliced bread

NOTE
You can jazz up this recipe by adding some spreads such as butter, peanut butter, jam or avocado. But, for now, that all just sounds like a bit much.

METHOD

Insert bread in toaster.

Toast to desired level of toastiness.

Nibble sporadically while sending various apology messages for last night's rambunctious behaviour.

BLOODY & BACON-Y MARY

SERVES 1

*Admittedly, hair of the dog might be delaying
the inevitable... But that's a problem for future you.*

INGREDIENTS

90 ml (3 fl oz) tomato juice
30–60 ml (2–3 fl oz) vodka (likely
  leftover on your coffee table)
splash lemon or lime juice
½ teaspoon dijon mustard
dash of Worcestershire sauce
dash of hot sauce (sriracha or
  Tabasco)
1 long slice cucumber
1 piece Candied beer bacon
  (optional, see page 102)
1 cherry tomato
1 coriander sprig (cilantro)

METHOD

Fill a cocktail shaker with ice and add the tomato
juice, vodka, lemon or lime juice, mustard and sauces,
and season generously with salt and pepper. Seal
and shake vigorously but briefly, then strain into
a tall glass half-filled with more ice. Garnish with
the cucumber, candied bacon (if using), tomato and
coriander.

Serve immediately, into self.

HOT MICHELADA

SERVES 2

You know those friends who came over last night and left
a six-pack of terrible Mexican beer in your fridge?
Here's a drink that'll put them to good use.

INGREDIENTS

1 tablespoon honey
3 tablespoons salt
½ teaspoon smoked paprika
pinch of chilli powder
30 ml (1 fl oz) freshly squeezed
    lime juice, plus extra lime slices,
    to garnish
15 ml (½ fl oz) worcestershire sauce
10 ml (¼ fl oz) hot sauce (or more,
    to taste)
330 ml (11 fl oz) Mexican lager
freshly ground black pepper,
    to garnish

METHOD

Spread the honey on a plate and dip the rims of two
chilled beer goblets in it.

On a separate plate, combine the salt, paprika and
chilli powder.

Dip the honeyed glass rims into the salt mix.

Combine the lime juice, sauces and a pinch of salt in
a cocktail shaker filled with ice and shake.

Strain into the goblets and add fresh ice.

Top with the beer. Add a sprinkling of black pepper
and garnish each with a lime slice. Be merry (again).

This drink is bitter.
Real bitter.
Which will probably pair with your current mood.

BITTER & BEER-Y MIMOSA

SERVES 1

INGREDIENTS

330 ml (11 fl oz) bottle hoppy IPA
    or double IPA
90 ml (3 fl oz) freshly squeezed
    grapefruit juice
grapefruit twist or wedge, to garnish

METHOD

Pour the beer into a chilled champagne flute, filling to around the two-thirds mark.

Add the grapefruit juice and stir gently to combine.

Garnish with a twist of grapefruit rind, or an entire wedge. Let the wild rumpus continue.

SPORTS DRANK

SERVES 1 SAD, SAD SOUL

We know that you weren't technically doing anything athletic last night, but a drinking session can often feel like a marathon.

INGREDIENTS

1 bottle colourful sports drank

METHOD

Position self on couch, or seat of similar comfortability.

Unscrew sippy-lid from bottle. Peel off protective film. Screw sippy-lid back onto bottle.

Sip periodically from bottle to restore your precious, precious electrolytes.

SPARKLING WATER

SERVES 1 TRULY LOST CAUSE

Can't keep anything down? Feel your optical nerve wanting to detach with every pound of the headache? There's only one recipe for you now...

INGREDIENTS

chilled tap water

METHOD

Place water in the bottle of your sparkling water maker.

Activate the bubbles.

Drink, hydrate and sleep. Tomorrow is another day.

INDEX

Well done, my friend.
If you've made it this far,
the worst is already over.

Published in 2019 by Smith Street Books
Melbourne | Australia
smithstreetbooks.com

ISBN: 978-1-925418-99-6

Publisher: Paul McNally
Project editors: Hannah Koelmeyer & Patrick Boyle
Introductory text: Patrick Boyle
Recipe Development: Aisling Coughlan, Caroline Griffiths, Lucy Heaver,
    Hannah Koelmeyer, Dave Adams, Sue Herold & Jane O'Shannessy
Proofreader: Lucy Heaver, Tusk studio
Design concept: Stephanie Spartels
Design layout: Megan Ellis
Stylists: Billy Law, Stephanie Stamatis & Vicki Valsamis
Food preparation: Janine Coster, Aisling Coughlan, Jemima Good, Caroline Griffiths,
    Sebastian Nichols, Jane O'Shannessy, Emma Roocke & Sebastien Zinzan.

Printed & bound in China by C&C Offset Printing Co., Ltd.

Book 81
10 9 8 7 6 5 4 3 2 1

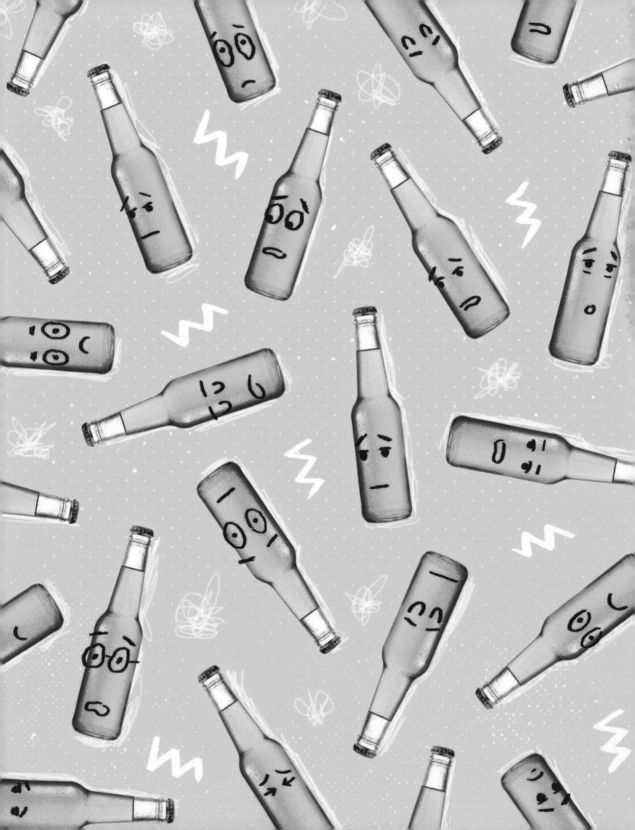